ideals®
EASTER
Vol. 48, No. 2

Publisher, Patricia A. Pingry
Editor, Nancy J. Skarmeas
Editorial Assistant, LaNita Kirby
Art Director, Patrick McRae

ISBN 0-8249-1089-3

IDEALS—Vol. 48, No. 2 March MCMXCI IDEALS (ISSN 0019-137X) is published eight times a year: February, March, May, June, August, September, November, December by IDEALS PUBLISHING CORPORATION, P.O. Box 148000, Nashville, Tenn. 37214. Second-class postage paid at Nashville, Tennessee, and additional mailing offices. Copyright © MCMXCI by IDEALS PUBLISHING CORPORATION. POSTMASTER: Send address changes to Ideals, Post Office Box 148000, Nashville, Tenn. 37214-8000. All rights reserved. Title IDEALS registered U.S. Patent Office.

SINGLE ISSUE—$4.95
ONE-YEAR SUBSCRIPTION—eight consecutive issues as published—$19.95
TWO-YEAR SUBSCRIPTION—sixteen consecutive issues as published—$35.95
Outside U.S.A., add $6.00 per subscription year for postage and handling.

ACKNOWLEDGMENTS

A PRAYER IN SPRING by Robert Frost: from *THE POETRY OF ROBERT FROST*, edited by Edward Connery Latham. Copyright 1934, © 1969 by Holt, Rinehart and Winston. Copyright © 1962 by Robert Frost, Reprinted by permission of Henry Holt and Company, Inc.; MY COMMITMENT by Angela Gall: Reprinted from *THROUGH TINTED PANES*, Copyright 1964 by Angela Gall: Used by permission of the author; PLANT A GARDEN by Edgar A. Guest: Used by permission of the estate; GOD, WHO HATH MADE THE DAISIES, by E. P. Hood: Reprinted from *OUR HOLIDAYS IN POETRY*, Copyright 1929 by H. W. Wilson Company: Used by permission; EASTER IN NEW ENGLAND, by Rose Koralewsky: Reprinted from *NEW ENGLAND HERITAGE AND OTHER POEMS*, Copyright 1949 by Bruce Humphries, Inc.: Used by permission of BRANDEN PUBLISHING, Boston; WHITE EASTER by Edgar Daniel Kramer: Used by permission of the estate's trustee; Excerpts from the book *STILLMEADOW DAYBOOK* by Gladys Taber: Copyright © 1955 by Gladys Taber. Copyright © renewed 1983 by Constance Taber Colby. Reprinted by permission of Harper Collins Publishers. Our sincere thanks to the following whose addresses we were unable to locate: Lela Bernard for NATURE'S RESURRECTION; Dorothy H. Cross for CONSOLATION; Ruth Linnea Erickson for PSALM OF SPRING, reprinted from HOMESPUN VERSE, copyright 1956; Jessie Rose Gates for LORD, MAKE ME STRONG; May Smith White for WHERE TULIPS FLOWER and EASTER'S EARLY DAWN; and Edwin C. Young for BE GLAD, ITS EASTER DAY.

Four-color separations by Rayson Films, Inc., Waukesha, Wisconsin

Printing by The Banta Company, Menasha, Wisconsin

The paper used in this publication meets the minimum requirements of American National Standard for Information Sciences—Permanence of Paper for Printed Library Materials, ANSI Z39.48-1984.

Unsolicited manuscripts will not be returned without a self-addressed stamped envelope.

Cover Photo
LILY AND STAINED GLASS
Fred Sieb

Inside Front Cover Inside Back Cover
THE LAST SUPPER HE IS RISEN
George Hinke   George Hinke

Psalm of Spring

Ruth L. Erikson

Nature robed in spring
    green awakens
To warming skies; and rising up
    she shakes
The last brown leaf
    from off the stubborn oak,
Then gently blows away
    the drifts that choke
Young greening fingers
    breaking through the sod
To lift a song of silent
    praise to God.

Standing ankle deep
    within a cup
Of budding flowers,
    Spring reaches up.
Refreshed with sleep,
    she stretches flowing limbs
Where nesting friends are singing
    joyful hymns,
Each lovely tree a green
    cathedral where
The leaves are still half-folded
    as in prayer.

TULIP IN SPRING SNOW
Larry Lefever/Grant Heilman Photography

BUTTERCUPS
Ina Mackey, Photographer

IT'S SPRING

Elisabeth Weaver Winstead

Tall reeds now cease their rattling sound,
Soft tracks appear on rain-soft ground.
In whistling tunes, the peepers sing:
Small messengers, announcing spring.

CROCUSES
Adam Jones Photography

In rainbow gleams on meadow's edge,
The crocus blooms beneath the hedge.
Gold daffodils are peeping up
Beside the tulip's glowing cup.

Enchanted by this green-sweet land,
I, spellbound, on my doorstep stand.
My heart in waves of joy takes wing,
At last I know—It's spring! It's spring!

Photo Overleaf
PINK DOGWOOD
AT BILTMORE ESTATE
Asheville, North Carolina
Tom Algire Photography

A Prayer in Spring

Robert Frost

Oh, give us pleasure in the flowers today;
And give us not to think so far away
As the uncertain harvest; keep us here
All simply in the springing of the year.

Oh, give us pleasure in the orchard white,
Like nothing else by day, like ghosts by night;
And make us happy in the happy bees,
The swarm dilating round the perfect trees.

And make us happy in the darting bird
That suddenly above the bees is heard,
The meteor that thrusts with needle bill,
And off a blossom in mid-air stands still.

For this is love and nothing else is love,
The which it is reserved for God above
To sanctify to what far ends He will,
But which it only needs that we fulfill.

Spring Is

I love to feel the wind running
    its fingers through my hair;
The gentle touch reminds me
    that God is always there.

I love to see the vibrant shades
    of green upon the tree;
Its graceful shape and strength of trunk
    bring me to bended knee.

I love to hear the music of a
    gurgling, gushing stream
As it surges o'er the rocks,
    praise of God its constant theme.

I love the varied fragrance
    with which flowers fill the air;
Their perfumes mingle to the clouds
    and I bow my head in prayer.

I love the wonderful bounty of
    God's table that we share
In the food provided from the ground
    cultivated with care.

In all we touch or see or smell
    or taste or even hear,
God's presence is in each sense we have;
    I'm grateful: He is near!

Meg Evatt
Inman, South Carolina

Reflections

Beauty That Comes to One Unasked

Beauty that comes to one unasked
Is like a cooling shower
That washes away all pain;

Is like a bird singing in the night,
And a single flower
Blooming in a forgotten garden.

Harriette Eaton
Washington, D.C.

Editor's Note: Readers are invited to submit unpublished, original poetry, short anecdotes, and humorous reflections on life for possible publication in future *Ideals* issues. Please send copies only; manuscripts will not be returned. Writers receive $10 for each published submission. Send material to: "Readers' Reflections," Ideals Publishing Corporation, P.O. Box 140300, Nashville, TN 37214-0300.

The Senses

Spring is sunshine through my window.
It is dew dripping its quiet song to itself.
Spring is wind whispering its happy song.
It is love coming to be craved
        in the world again.
Spring is when life comes back
        to sing its peaceful song.
Spring is a wonderful, wonderful
        time of the year!

Alison Nunnally
Zephyr Cove, Nevada

My Commitment

Angela Gall

Who guides the season of the crocus,
Rose, and goldenrod;

Who brings to life the fallow field
And quickens verdant sod;

Who gives the songbird plain and wood,
And gull the rampant sea

Where waves foam in to lap the shore,
May have his way with me.

Photo Opposite
MID-CENTURY HYBRID LILY
S. Rennels/Grant Heilman Photography

April Promise

Mary E. Linton

I think the world was born
   one April day
With fragrant winds astir
   upon the deep,
With bursting blossoms and
   the first bright ray
Of sunlight bringing life
   to powers asleep.

Out of primeval fire,
   the earth we know
Blossomed with gentle warmth
   one April dawn,
Burst softly into Time
   as petals glow
With newborn rapture
   on the dew-kissed lawn.

And every year
   it celebrates anew,
Small candles with
   brightly colored flame.
Oh, happy birthday,
   all the world, to you!
What joy to be alive
   and call your name.
What joy to share with you
   another year
When blossoms rich
   with promise reappear.

APPLE BLOSSOMS
Hood River Valley, Oregon
Suzanne Clemenz Photography

WHERE TULIPS FLOWER

May Smith White

I saw her standing
   by the tulip bed—
Caressing snow-white
   blossoms as before.
She knows spring days
   of sun and rain have fed
The roots of tulips
   blooming at her door.
Each year it is the same
   with those who keep
Bright hopes with spring
   forever fresh and new.
And then in season
   they will come to reap
A harvest rich as
   prism-jeweled dew.

Life offers peace to those
   who know this plan.
A balm will come with every
   new-made day,
And such tranquility will
   cause the span
Of years to glow,
   as does each bright sun ray.
So might she who has known
   this holy hour,
Walk always where
   the lovely tulips flower.

April in Washington, D. C. : Cherry Blossom Time

Springtime visitors to Washington, D. C., owe a debt of gratitude to Mrs. William Howard Taft, a former First Lady with a habit of seeing things not as they always had been, but as she thought they should be. She was the first to ride beside her husband in the inaugural procession down Pennsylvania Avenue. She allowed her cow to graze on the White House lawn. And it was Mrs. Taft who first envisioned Japanese ornamental cherry trees blooming around Washington's Tidal Basin.

Somehow, the Japanese got word of Mrs. Taft's wish. In 1909 they sent a shipment of their prized *Yoshino* cherry tree saplings to the United States. The trees arrived safely in Washington, but Mrs. Taft's vision would have to wait. When the crates were opened, the Department of Agriculture declared them infested, and the trees were burned. Apologies were made, but it was not until three years later, in 1912, that the Japanese tried again to fulfill Mrs. Taft's wish. This time, 3,000 young trees, including twelve different varieties, arrived safely in Washington. Later that year, Mrs. Taft, accompanied by the wife of the Japanese ambassador, planted the first cherry tree on the Tidal Basin.

Nearly eighty years later, the cherry trees remain, and they are now as recognizable a part of the city's landscape as its many museums, monuments, and government buildings. The Capitol, one of our most beautiful cities in all seasons, is never more beautiful than during those few days in early April when the Japanese ornamental cherry trees explode into magnificent pink and white splendor.

Rimming the Tidal Basin and spilling out onto the grounds of the Washington Monument, over 3,000 cherry trees bloom simultaneously each spring, their multitudes of white and pale pink blossoms spreading a delicate gossamer over the city. The blossoms have no noticeable scent, but they lift a canopy of lace across the walkways of the basin, producing a magical atmosphere. From beneath this canopy the normally striking views of the city are intensified. The classic columns of the Jefferson Memorial are more brilliant than ever when framed by a border of blossoms, and the majestic Washington Monument seems built to rise from this sea of pink and white.

To be in Washington during cherry blossom time is truly an event for the soul; to be there during those few days when the blossoms are at their peak, however, is almost an accident. The city hosts an annual week-long Cherry Blossom Festival, usually the first week of April. Each year, visitors arrive on schedule. Unfortunately, nature pays no heed to the planners' schedule, and the days of the official celebration do not always coincide with the actual peak blooming period.

Not to be discouraged, the official festivities carry on, opening each year with the lighting of a twenty-ton, three-hundred-year-old Japanese Stone Lantern, another gift from the people of Japan. In the week that follows there are parades, floats, band competitions, sporting events, tea dances, concerts, and a black tie ball, all in honor of the beautiful trees and our friendship with their native country.

But the most glorious experience remains a simple, unofficial one: a quiet walk under the softly cascading cherry blossoms, stepping over the silky fallen petals, and pausing to view the historic city in its annual spring splendor. The trees are now so much a part of spring in Washington that it is hard to imagine a time before them; the beautiful pink and white blossoms are the perfect complement to the striking structures that are the city's trademark. Today, Mrs. Taft seems less a non-conformist than a woman of vision. In a city known for its monuments, these trees are perfectly at home, a living memorial both to a friendship between countries half a world apart and to the possibilities of seeing our world as we'd like it to be.

Photos courtesy of the National Park Service.

19

Nature's Resurrection

Lela Bernard

The orchards resembled forgotten
Ghost towns, leafless trees in frozen rows,
Lifeless arms outstretched as if pleading
For relief from the cold winter snows.
Here and there ragged bird's nests cling
Tenaciously to limbs cold and bare.
A withered leaf, reluctant to leave
Mother tree, shivered in winter air.

Then beneath the topsoil new life stirred and
Surged through dormant roots. Glorious spring
Whispered a message that winter cold
Would soon be gone and birds would sing,
Because there would be resurrection
Of nature's beautiful, sleeping things.
Trees would be transformed into living
Bouquets with blossoms like angel wings.
And then the harvest, ripe fruit
Blushing from kisses by summer's sun,
Bearing seeds to insure their rebirth:
Divine plan for Nature's resurrection.

Photo Opposite
THE CAPITOL
Gottlieb Hampfler, Photographer

FROM MY G·A·R·D·E·N JOURNAL

Deana Deck

Japanese Cherry Trees

When I was a child, our family lived for a time near Washington, D.C., and each spring we came to expect waves of company as relatives and friends from faraway places streamed into town just in time for what was invariably referred to as "The Viewing."

This annual rite of spring, trekking to the Tidal Basin to view the glorious display of the Japanese cherry trees, remains permanently etched in my mind.

After the spring visit, however, all interest in the trees ceased. No one ever suggested going back in summer to eat the cherries. This puzzled my childish sense of priorities. To me, one blossom was the same as the next, but no flower could rival the taste of a freshly picked cherry.

As it happened, though, I got my fill of cherries each summer. Not too far from where we lived was a home with an enormous black cherry tree in the front yard. The tree was as large as an oak and produced bushels of fruit each year. During cherry season my friends and I would ride over on our bicycles, intent on juicy mouthfuls of sweet cherries. Weary of losing entire crops of cherries to the birds each year, the elderly lady who owned the tree had come up with a most satisfactory solution. She would hand out berry baskets to any neighborhood child with a taste for cherries, and we were free to climb the tree and stuff ourselves as we filled our baskets with cherries.

When we had eaten our fill, we would climb down and hand over the full baskets to the smiling owner of the tree. Each spring, on those trips around the Tidal Basin, I would dream of that huge fruit-filled cherry tree.

Eventually, I learned that flowering cherry trees and fruiting cherry trees are quite different, and that the beautiful blossoms of the one could be as pleasurable as the delicious fruit of the other. Today, I know that if you decide to add cherry blossoms to your springtime, you must choose either abundant fruit or spectacular blossoms. You cannot have both.

If you select blooms, you are at the mercy of the weather, since the flowering cherry is one of the earliest spring-blooming ornamentals and is highly susceptible to late frosts. If you select cherries, prepare to battle the birds—as well as the weather—for each piece of fruit you harvest.

Since cherries are so abundantly available in produce markets each summer, and since the dream of growing your own fruit can easily turn into the nightmare of fruit viruses, scale, insects, birds, and small cherry-thieving children, my advice is to concentrate on what the Japanese refer to as the *sakura,* or the soul, of the cherry: its incomparable blossom.

The Japanese began cultivating the flowering cherry tree over one thousand years ago. Most of the three thousand trees presented to the United States in 1912 by the mayor of Tokyo—those now flowering around the Tidal Basin—are *Yoshino* cherries. The *Yoshino* produces single, fragrant, pale pink blossoms that eventually fade to white.

Another variety is the *Kwanzan.* These have the added virtue of being heat tolerant enough to survive as far south as Zone 9. The *Kwanzan* produces large clusters of double pink flowers. The *Shiro-fugan* starts with pink buds that open to white blossoms and then fade back to pink again. All three are widely available in nurseries and are recommended by the National Arboretum as being fairly reliable in a home landscape.

Flowering cherries should be planted in full sun for the best blooms, although they seem to live a little longer when partial shade is available in hot weather. They should be planted in slightly acidic soil while dormant and watered well for the first year or so.

Since I live in a Zone 6 climate that is frequently host to late frosts, I try to spare myself as much heartache as possible by not growing these flowering beauties. But for those in slightly warmer regions, the flowering cherry can be one of the most rewarding of garden projects. I find evidence of this on my occasional springtime visits to my brother, who still lives near Washington, as we stroll the Tidal Basin together in wonderment.

Deana Deck lives in Nashville, Tennessee, where her garden column is a regular feature in the Tennessean.

Spring Morning

Alice M. Barber

I hadn't meant to stay so long.
I just came out to see
The nest of baby robins
In the chinaberry tree.

But then, a bright winged butterfly
Came drifting up the way,
And a small green frog by the water's edge;
Well, I never meant to stay.

I know I should be doing
At least a hundred things,
But have you ever noticed
A bird's throat when it sings?

Or watched the way the wind
Comes briskly up the road,
And pausing for a moment
Sets down for you its load

Of wild rose scent and sweet grass
And pines warmed by the sun?
On such a lovely day as this,
How can my work get done?

HERB GARDEN
Pennsylvania
Grant Heilman Photography

A SLICE OF LIFE

—Edgar A. Guest—

Plant a Garden

If your purse no longer bulges
    and you've lost your golden treasure,
If at times you think you're lonely
    and have hungry grown for pleasure,
Don't sit by your hearth and grumble,
    don't let mind and spirit harden.
If it's thrills of joy you wish for,
    get to work and plant a garden!

If it's drama that you sigh for,
    plant a garden and you'll get it.
You will know the thrill of battle
    fighting foes that will beset it.
If you long for entertainment and
    for pageantry most glowing,
Plant a garden, and this summer spend
    your time with green things growing.

If it's comradeship you sigh for,
    learn the fellowship of daisies.
You will come to know your neighbor
    by the blossoms that he raises;
If you'd get away from boredom
    and find new delights to look for,
Learn the joy of budding pansies
    which you've kept a special nook for.

If you ever think of dying
    and you fear to wake tomorrow,
Plant a garden! It will cure you
    of your melancholy sorrow.
Once you've learned to know peonies,
    petunias, and roses,
You will find that every morning
    some new happiness discloses.

Edgar A. Guest began his illustrious career in 1895 at the age of fourteen when his work first appeared in the Detroit Free Press. *His column was syndicated in over 300 newspapers, and he became known as "The Poet of the People."*

EASTER BELLS

Carice Williams

The Easter Bells ring out today
To tell the world it's Easter Day.
The earth in all its newness glows
Because this day our Lord arose.

The Easter bells chime out again
A happy message to all men.
Gone are pain and death and gloom:
Our Lord has risen from his tomb!

Country CHRONICLE
Gladys Taber

April

Early morning is like a pink pearl now that April is here. The first lilacs are budding over the white picket fence in the Quiet Garden; crocus, daffodils, white and purple grape hyacinths repeat the magic of spring. Surely never was spring so wonderful, such a miracle! For it seems only yesterday that drifts piled high in the little garden as I made my mittened and booted way to the kennel. My heart remembers this with surprise as I examine the delicate papery bud tips on my favorite King Alfred white daffodils.

The King Alfred has a silvery cup with a faint glow in the heart almost like old polished ivory. I really wonder why it was named King Alfred—not that it isn't a royal flower but that it

30

doesn't look masculine. It reminds me of a tall and mediaeval Princess robed in ivory velvet.

The early flowers have a special beauty—I always shake with excitement when I find the first clump of snowdrops, fragile, pearl-pure, bending their heads lightly toward the icy dark ground. Crocus makes rainbow patches all over the yard; scilla looks like bits of the sky nipped out and scattered down.

The sun rises around half past five in early April, and the mornings are so fresh and still. I like to get up and dash to the garden and see what the rhubarb is doing and then carry my breakfast tray to a sheltered sunny corner by the well. I like to eat outdoors even if I have to wear a sweater and Jill says I will eat out even if I have to wear mittens while I cut my bacon.

White clouds scud across the sky, the meadow has a faint haze of green, the wild pear is blossoming in the old orchard up the hill. The pure white blossoms give the countryside a look of having silver fountains here and there. The strange upright growth-pattern of the pear is so distinctive, somehow proud. The apple tree is graceful and charming and poetic, but the pear tree seems to have such integrity, pointing firmly up to the sky.

MICHELLE WITH BUNNY
Dick Dietrich Photography

A Child's Easter Song

Margaret Widdemer

The world has come awake
And will be lovely soon
With warm sunlight at noon
And ripples in the lake.

Now soon the ground will flower
And scarlet tulips grow
Down borders in a row
All opened in an hour;

For where the earth was brown
The pointed leaves of green
Reach out, and there are seen
Red flowers folded down:

The snows have gone away
And all the little birds
Sing songs that need no words,
For this is Easter Day.

EASTER BASKET AND WILDFLOWERS
Mrs. Kevin Scheibel, Photographer

Be Glad, It's Easter Day

Edwin C. Young

Be glad, winter has waned,
    springtime is now at hand,
Each meadow and each country lane
    will soon be green again;
The buds will burst on every tree,
    the birds will sing so gay,
Join with harmony in their glee,
    be glad, it's Easter Day.

We should rejoice on Easter Day,
    for many, many things,
But to Christ we should kneel and pray,
    for the blessings Easter brings,
For Christ in His resurrection,
    in love did pave the way,
For all the world's salvation,
    be glad! It's Easter Day!

God, Who Hath Made the Daisies

E. P. Hood

God, who hath made the daisies
   and every lovely thing,
He will accept our praises
   and harken while we sing.
He says though we are simple,
   though ignorant we be,
"Suffer the little children,
   and let them come to Me."

Though we are young and simple,
   in praise we may be bold;
The children in the temple
   He heard in days of old.
And if our hearts are humble,
   He says to you and me,
"Suffer the little children,
   and let them come to Me."

He sees the bird that wingeth
   its way over earth and sky;
He hears the lark that singeth
   up in the heaven high;
But sees the hearts' low breathings
   and says (well pleased to see),
"Suffer the little children,
   and let them come to Me."

Therefore we will come near Him,
   and solemnly we'll sing;
No cause to shrink or fear Him,
   we'll make our voices ring;
For in our temple speaking,
   He says to you and me,
"Suffer the little children,
   and let them come to Me."

Art from *THE EASTER STORY*, written and illustrated by Carol Heyer, Copyright ©
1990 by Ideals Publishing Corporation, Nashville, Tennessee

And they brought
young children to him,
that he should touch them:
and his disciples rebuked
those that brought them.

But when Jesus saw it,
he was much displeased,
and said unto them,
Suffer the little children
to come unto me,
and forbid them not:
for of such is the
kingdom of God.

Mark 10:13-14

Easter's Early Dawn

May Smith White

The quietness I find here
Renders a silent symphony . . .
But only those who listen
Will share in these rich blessings.

The birds now have grown muted and still,
Each one reflecting a deep kinship
With this Holy Hour.

White Easter

Edgar Daniel Kramer

Though all of the world was a sepulcher
Under a bleak, gray sky,
Empty and dead in a shroud of snow,
While the mournful winds swept by;
Though all the world was a sepulcher,
Sullen and cold, dark,
The Eastertide brought joy to me,
For Christ rose in my heart!

German Easter Braid

Holidays like Easter bring out the best in bread bakers around the world. In many countries, festive sweet breads are an important part of the Easter celebration, and cooks often spend hours preparing their traditional holiday delicacies. Although schedules today do not allow for a whole day in the kitchen, bread baking can still be a part of a special Easter feast. A sweet yeast bread like the German Easter Braid is quick and easy to make when you start with a hot roll mix. For an Easter brunch, fill the center of the braid with colored hard-cooked eggs and let it serve as a festive holiday centerpiece.

1	16 ounce package hot roll mix
½	cup golden raisins
1	teaspoon grated lemon peel
1	cup water heated to 110° to 120°F
2	tablespoons margarine or butter
¼	teaspoon almond or anise extract
1	egg
2	tablespoons sliced almonds
	Colored hard-boiled eggs

Honey Butter

¼	cup honey
⅓	cup butter or margarine, softened

In large bowl, combine yeast from foil packet with flour mixture; mix well. Add raisins, lemon peel, hot water, 2 tablespoons margarine, almond extract, and egg; stir until dough pulls cleanly away from sides of the bowl. Turn dough out onto lightly floured surface. With greased or floured hands, shape dough into ball. Knead dough for 5 minutes until smooth. Cover dough with large bowl; let rest 5 minutes. Grease large cookie sheet.

Divide dough into 3 equal parts; on lightly floured surface, shape each into a 22-inch rope. Braid ropes loosely from center to each end, overlapping every other rope. Place on greased cookie sheet and shape into a circle. Pinch ends together to seal. Cover loosely with a plastic wrap and cloth towel. Let rise in warm place (80° to 85°) 30 minutes.

Heat oven to 375°. Uncover dough. Bake at 375° for 14 to 18 minutes or until golden brown. In small bowl, combine honey and butter; blend well. Brush 2 tablespoons Honey Butter over braid immediately after removing from oven. Arrange almonds on braid. Return to oven and bake an additional 5 minutes. Remove from cookie sheet; cool on wire rack. Serve remaining Honey Butter as accompaniment to bread. Garnish center of bread with colored hard-cooked eggs. (Store eggs in refrigerator.)

Makes 1 loaf.

NUTRITIONAL ANALYSIS

Serving size: ⅛ of recipe.

Calories	250	Protein	8%
Protein	5g	Vitamin A	6%
Carbohydrates	41g	Vitamin C	*
Fat	8g	Thiamine	15%
Sodium	340mg	Riboflavin	15%
Potassium	115mg	Niacin	10%
		Calcium	*
		Iron	8%

Percent U. S. RDA per serving:

*Contains less than 2% of the U. S. RDA of this nutrient.

Photo Opposite
GERMAN EASTER BRAID
Photo Courtesy of the Pillsbury Company
Recipe Copyright 1990, Pillsbury Classic Cookbook,
The Pillsbury Company

EASTER MORNING

Edmund Spenser

Most glorious Lord of life, that on this day
Didst make thy triumph over death and sin,
And having harrowed hell, didst bring away
Captivity thence captive, us to win;
This joyous day, dear Lord, with joy begin,
And grant that we, for whom thou didst die,
Being with thy dear blood clean washed
   from sin,
May likewise love thee for the same again:
And for thy sake, that all like dear didst buy,
With love may one another entertain.
So let us love, dear love, like as we ought;
Love is the lesson which our Lord has taught.

THE REVIVAL

Henry Vaughan

Unfold, unfold! take in his light,
Who makes thy cares more short than night.
The joys, with which his day-star rise,
He deals to all, but drowsy eyes:
And what the men of this world miss,
Some drops and dews of future bliss.
Hark! how his winds have changed their note,
And with warm whispers call thee out.
The frosts are past, the storms are gone:
And backward life at last comes on.
The lofty groves in express joys
Reply above the turtle's voice,
And here in dust and dirt, O here
The lilies of his love appear!

CRAFTWORKS

Pysanky: Hand-Painted Ukranian Easter Eggs

Each year before Easter, Dianne Mezger goes into what may best be described as an "egg decorating frenzy." Her hand-painted eggs have sold in gift shops and at art fairs, but Dianne finds greatest pleasure in the creative process, and in giving the eggs, called *pysanky,* to friends and family.

To be a master at this art requires time and dedication. Still, simple, beautiful *pysanky* are within the reach of any beginner. It is best to start with the drop-pull method described below. With time and patience, extraordinary results can be achieved. And this is an inexpensive hobby: Dianne estimates that she has spent less than $100 in seventeen years!

Materials Needed:

Smooth, fresh eggs at room temperature
Writing tools (straight pins stuck into a dowel, cork, or pencil eraser)
Wax (equal amounts beeswax and paraffin)
Wax warmer (candle heated container)
Egg dyes (prepared according to package instructions in containers large enough to submerge eggs)
Paper tissues or soft absorbent cloth

Step One: Preparing the Eggs

Dianne recommends "blowing" your eggs before painting. Use a long pin to make a tiny hole at each end; the hole should be a bit larger at the bottom. Pierce and break the yolk with the long pin. Shake to mix the inner contents. Over a bowl or sink, blow through the smaller hole to force the contents out of the larger opening. Rinse the shell and prop on an egg carton to dry.

Step Two: Creating the Design

(*Tip*: Practice your design on paper before applying wax to the egg.) Melt the wax. Working quickly to prevent the wax from hardening, dip the pinhead into melted wax and touch it to the egg to create your design. The pinhead touched to the egg will form a small dot. To make a tear drop shape, draw the pinhead along the surface of the egg. These two shapes may be used in different combinations to make a variety of designs.

Step Three: Adding Color

One to three colors are usually used for each egg. Always progress from the lightest to the darkest dye color. When the complete wax design has been applied, place the egg in the first dye solution. Turn gently in the solution several times until desired color is reached (approximately 10 to 30 minutes). The longer the egg remains in the dye, the deeper the color will be. Remove the egg and blot dry with tissue or cloth.

Once the egg is dry, add additional wax designs and repeat color process with darker dye.

Step Four: Finishing

After the final dye bath, remove the wax by holding the egg, a small section at a time, against the side of the candle flame for no more than five seconds. As soon as the section appears wet, blot with a clean, soft cloth. Continue until all the wax is removed. Do not hold the egg over the tip of flame, as carbon will collect and darken your design. Eggs may be preserved with varnish.

Karen Hodge writes articles, essays, and educational materials from her home in Antioch, Tennessee. Dianne Mezger paints eggs at her home in Klamath Falls, Orgeon. They have been friends since 1961.

Photo Opposite
PYSANKY IN BASKET
Gerald Koser

COLLECTOR'S CORNER

Ukranian Painted Easter Eggs

Karen S. Hodge

Dianne Mezger remembers the first time she saw Ukranian painted eggs. She could think of nothing else for days. "They were like jewels. I couldn't believe that anyone could create them free-hand," she says.

Since that first sighting seventeen years ago, Dianne has learned the ancient folk art of painting eggs in this style. In the process, she has also learned about the folklore, legend, and religious symbolism of this beautiful collectible.

The common eggs, which Ukranians call *pysanky,* are created with a batik-like method using wax and dyes. Both the designs and the colors are symbolic. Some designs can be traced back to pagan times, but with the arrival of Christianity in the Ukraine, most of the pagan symbols took on new, Christian meanings. What makes these eggs such a fascinating collectible are the stories told by the symbols that make up each design. The faith and personality of the artist are reflected in her choice of color and symbol. Some of the most frequently used symbols are described in the following chart.

A leaf or flower suggests life and growth.

Pine needles represent youth and health.

The fish is an ancient symbol for Christ.

Deer and horses represent wealth and prosperity.

Birds represent fertility and the fulfillment of wishes.

Grapes symbolize the "good fruits" of Christian life.

A butterfly is a symbol of the resurrection.

A ribbon or belt around the egg symbolizes eternity.

Dots or small circles represent stars or constellations.

A sieve or a net suggests fishing.

Small baskets or triangles symbolize the Holy Trinity.

Ladders suggest prayer.

An eight-pointed star is an ancient symbol for Christ.

A cross signifies the suffering and resurrection of Christ.

The oldest *pysanky* were made with only two colors. As the peasant women learned to make more and more dyes out of natural substances, the range of colors grew. Recipes for dyes became guarded family secrets, passed down from one generation to the next.

Vivid, bold colors were and still are used. There are no pale pastels to be found on these eggs. White is representative of purity. Yellow on *pysanky* represents successful harvest and wisdom; green is the color of rebirth and spring. Some colors have a variety of symbolic meanings. Blue, for instance, represents sky, air, and good health; and orange can be used to reflect both endurance and ambition.

The art form is also rich in legend. One of the most often repeated stories of *pysanky*'s origin is that when Mary pleaded with Pontius Pilate to spare her son's life, she offered him some colored eggs. Her tears, which fell on the eggs, formed bright dots. The eggs made by Ukranian women thereafter were in memory of Mary's grief.

Pysanky can be found in gift shops throughout the United States and Canada, especially around Easter time. They can also be seen in art museums where folk art is on display. It is wise to invest in egg cups or holders to display your eggs, for they are as delicate as they are beautiful. Wooden, brass, or lucite stands are available at gift shops and import houses.

Prices for these eggs vary, but for the most part they are very affordable. For collectors whose pocketbooks don't allow for acquisition of a fabulous Faberge jewelled egg, the jewel-like Ukranian egg—rich with history and tradition—is a wonderful alternative.

THE TRIUMPHANT ENTRY

And when they drew nigh unto Jerusalem, and were come to Bethphage, unto the Mount of Olives, then sent Jesus two disciples, saying unto them, Go into the village over against you, and straightaway ye shall find an ass tied, and a colt with her: loose them, and bring them unto me. And if any man say ought unto you, ye shall say, The Lord hath need of them, and straightaway he will send them.

All this was done, that it might be fulfilled which was spoken by the prophet, saying, Tell ye the daughter of Sion, Behold, thy king cometh unto thee, meek, and sitting upon an ass.

And the disciples went, and did as Jesus commanded them, and brought the ass, and the colt, and put on them their clothes, and they set him thereon. And a very great multitude spread their garments in the way; others cut down branches from the trees, and strewed them in the way. And the multitudes that went before, and that followed, cried, saying, Hosanna to the son of David: Blessed is he that cometh in the name of the Lord; Hosanna in the highest.

And Jesus went into the temple of God, and cast out all them that sold and bought in the temple, and overthrew the tables of the money changers, and the seats of them that sold doves, and he said unto them, It is written, My house shall be called the house of prayer, but ye have made it a den of thieves. And the blind and the lame came to him in the temple; and he healed them. And when the chief priests and scribes saw the wonderful things that he did, and the children crying in the temple, and saying, Hosanna to the son of David, they were sore displeased.

Matthew 21: 1-9; 12-15

Opposite
PALM SUNDAY
St. Philip Neri, Chicago, Illinois
The Crosiers/Gene Plaisted, OSC, Photographer

THE LAST SUPPER

Now the first day of the feast of unleavened bread the disciples came to Jesus, saying unto him, Where wilt thou that we prepare for you to eat the passover? And he said, Go into the city to such a man, and say to him, The Master saith, My time is at hand; I will keep the passover at thy house with my disciples. And the disciples did as Jesus had appointed them; and they made ready the passover.

Now when the even was come, he sat down with the twelve. And as they did eat, he said, Verily I say unto you, that one of you shall betray me. And they were exceeding sorrowful, and began every one of them to say unto him, Lord, is it I? And he answered and said, He that dippeth his hand with me in the dish, the same shall betray me. The Son of man goeth as it is written of him: but woe unto that man by whom the Son of man is betrayed! It had been good for that man that he had not been born.

And as they were eating, Jesus took bread, and blessed it, and brake it, and gave it to the disciples, and said, Take, eat; this is my body. And he took the cup, and gave thanks, and gave it to them, saying, Drink ye all of it for this is my blood of the new testament which is shed for many for the remission of sins. But I say unto you, I will not drink henceforth of this fruit of the vine, until that day when I drink it new with you in my Father's kingdom. And when they had sung an hymn, they went out into the Mount of Olives.

Matthew 26: 17-24; 26-30

Opposite
THE LAST SUPPER
St. Agnes, St. Paul, Minnesota
The Crosiers/Gene Plaisted, OSC, Photographer

THE GARDEN

Then cometh Jesus with them unto a place called Gethsemane, and saith unto the disciples, sit ye here while I go and pray yonder. And he took with him Peter and the two sons of Zebedee and began to be sorrowful and very heavy. Then he saith unto them, My soul is exceeding sorrowful, even unto death; tarry ye here and watch with me.

And he went a little farther and fell on his face, and prayed, saying, O my Father, if it be possible, let this cup pass from me: nevertheless, not as I will, but as thou wilt. And he cometh unto the disciples and findeth them asleep, and saith unto Peter, What could ye not watch with me one hour? He went away again the second time, and prayed, saying, O my Father, if this cup may not pass away from me, except I drink it, thy will be done. And he came and found them asleep again; for their eyes were heavy. And he left them and went away again, and prayed the third time, saying the same words.

Then cometh he to his disciples, and saith unto them, Sleep now and take your rest, behold, the hour is at hand, and the Son of man is betrayed into the hands of sinners. And while he yet spake, lo, Judas, one of the twelve, came, and with him a great multitude with swords and staves, from the chief priests and elders of the people. Now he that betrayed him gave them a sign, saying, Whomsoever I shall kiss, the same is he: hold him fast. And forthwith he came to Jesus, and said, Hail, master, and kissed him. And they that had laid hold on Jesus led him away to Caiaphas the high priest, where the scribes and elders were assembled.

Matthew 26: 36-40; 42-45; 47-49; 57

Opposite
JESUS IN GETHSEMANE
St. Helena's, Minneapolis, Minnesota
The Crosiers/Gene Plaisted, OSC, Photographer

THE WAY OF THE CROSS

When the morning was come, all the chief priests and elders of the people took counsel against Jesus to put him to death: And when they had bound him, they led him away, and delivered him to Pontius Pilate the governor.

And Jesus stood before the governor: and the governor asked him, saying, Art thou the King of the Jews? And Jesus said unto him, Thou sayest. And when he was accused of the chief priests and elders, he answered nothing. Then Pilate said to him, Hearest thou not how many things they witness against thee? And he answered to him never a word; insomuch that the governor marvelled greatly.

Now at that feast the governor was wont to release unto the people a prisoner, whom they would. And they had then a notable prisoner, called Barabbas. Therefore, when they were gathered together, Pilate said unto them, Whom will ye that I release unto you? Barabbas, or Jesus which is called Christ? For he knew that for envy they had delivered him. The governor answered and said unto them, Whether of the twain will ye that I release unto you? They said Barabbas. Pilate saith unto them, What shall I do then with Jesus which is called Christ? They all say unto him, Let him be crucified.

Then the soldiers of the governor took Jesus into the common hall, and gathered unto him the whole band of soldiers. And they stripped him, and put on him a scarlet robe. And, after that they had mocked him, they took the robe off from him, and put his own raiment on him, and led him away to crucify him.

Matthew 27:1-2; 11-18; 21-22; 27-28; 31

THE CRUCIFIXION

And when they were come unto a place called Golgotha, that is to say, a place of a skull, they gave him vinegar to drink mingled with gall; and when he had tasted thereof, he would not drink. And they crucified him, and parted his garments, casting lots: that it might be fulfilled which was spoken by the prophet, They parted my garments among them, and upon my vesture did they cast lots.

And sitting down, they watched him there; and set up over his head his accusation, written, THIS IS JESUS THE KING OF THE JEWS.

Then were there two thieves crucified with him, one on the right hand and another on the left. And they that passed by reviled him, wagging their heads, And saying, Thou that destroyest the temple, and buildest it in three days, save thyself. If thou be the Son of God, come down from the cross. Likewise, also the chief priests mocking him, with the scribes and elders, said, He saved others; himself he cannot save. If he be the King of Israel, let him now come down from the cross, and we will believe him. He trusted in God; let him deliver him now, if he will have him: for he said, I am the son of God.

And about the ninth hour Jesus cried with a loud voice, saying, Eli, Eli, lama sa bach'thani? that is to say, My God, My God, why hast thou forsaken me?

Jesus, when he had cried again with a loud voice, yielded up the ghost. And behold, the vail of the temple was rent in twain from the top to the bottom; and the earth did quake, and the rocks rent.

Matthew 27: 33-43; 46; 50-51

THE ANGEL OF THE LORD

Now when the centurion, and they that were with him, watching Jesus, saw the earthquake, and those things that were done, they feared greatly, saying, Truly this was the son of God. And many women were there beholding afar off, which followed Jesus from Galilee, ministering unto him: Among which was Mary Magdalene, and Mary the mother of James and Joses, and the mother of Zebedee's children. When the even was come, there came a rich man of Arimathea named Joseph, who also himself was Jesus' disciple: He went to Pilate, and begged the body of Jesus. Then Pilate commanded the body to be delivered.

And when Joseph had taken the body, he wrapped it in a clean linen cloth, and laid it in his own new tomb, which he had hewn out in the rock: and he rolled a great stone to the door of the sepulchre, and departed. And there was Mary Magdalene, and the other Mary, sitting over against the sepulchre.

In the end of the sabbath, as it began to dawn toward the first day of the week, came Mary Magdalene and the other Mary to see the sepulchre. And, behold, there was a great earthquake; for the angel of the Lord descended from heaven, and came and rolled back the stone from the door and sat upon it. His countenance was like lightning, and his raiment white as snow: And the angel answered and said unto the women, Fear not ye: for I know that ye seek Jesus, which was crucified. He is not here: for he is risen, as he said. Come, see the place where the Lord lay. And go quickly, and tell his disciples that he is risen from the dead; and, behold, he goeth before you into Galilee; there shall ye see him: lo, I have told you.

Matthew 27: 54-61; 28:1-3; 5-7

Opposite
EASTER ANGEL
United Church of Christ, Falcon Heights, Minnesota
The Crosiers/Gene Plaisted, OSC, Photographer

THE RESURRECTION

And they departed quickly from the sepulchre with fear and great joy; and did run to bring his disciples word. And as they went to tell his disciples, behold, Jesus met them, saying, All hail, and they came and held him by the feet, and worshiped him. Then said Jesus unto them, Be not afraid: go tell my brethren that they go into Galilee, and there shall they see me.

Now when they were going, behold, some of the watch came into the city, and shewed unto the chief priests all the things that were done. And when they were assembled with the elders, and had taken counsel, they gave large money unto the soldiers, saying, Say ye, His disciples came by night, and stole him away while we slept. And if this come to the governor's ears, we will persuade him, and secure you. So they took the money, and did as they were taught.

Then the eleven disciples went away into Galilee, into a mountain where Jesus had appointed them. And when they saw him, they worshiped him: but some doubted. And Jesus came and spake unto them, saying, All power is given unto me in heaven and in earth. Go ye therefore, and teach all nations, baptizing them in the name of the Father, and of the Son, and of the Holy Ghost: Teaching them to observe all things whatsoever I have commanded you: and, lo, I am with you alway, even unto the end of the world.

Matthew 28: 8-20

Opposite
EASTER MORNING
St. Vincent de Paul, Minneapolis, Minnesota
The Crosiers/Gene Plaisted, OSC, Photographer

THROUGH MY WINDOW
— Pamela Kennedy —

Mary of Magdala

There were those, she supposed, who would call her possessed still. They would say she was captivated by her adoration of this strange Galilean just as she had been earlier in her life by seven evil spirits.

But Mary knew the difference. In those years before Jesus touched her, she had been driven past insanity—unloved and cast away from "good people." Then Jesus had passed through her town, little Magdala, on the western shores of Galilee. She didn't remember much of the encounter except that his cool, firm hand had touched her and the evil spirits had departed. She could think and speak and dream her own dreams again, and she wanted nothing more than to follow the one who had healed her. If that was possession, so be it.

Mary had joined two other women who traveled with Jesus, cooking meals and washing clothes. Others might have considered it menial; she considered it a privilege. By their acts of simple service they were able to hear his every word.

Mary assumed it would be her vocation for as long as she lived. It had not occurred to her that he would die first. But here she stood, surrounded by the crowd. On the crest of the hill, Jesus hung, bleeding and dying. And Mary could do nothing. She wanted to pray, but could not remember the words. She wanted to comfort his mother, but could not think how.

Through the day she remained, absorbing every sight and sound. She saw the darkness wrap itself around the city like a shroud. She felt the clammy heat of noon and the tremble of the earth. She heard the cry, "It is finished!" and watched as they took him off the cross. She followed as Joseph of Arimathea carried the lifeless body to his own tomb. She wanted to help, to serve, but there was nothing to be done. Or was there?

The sky was beginning to dim as she hurried to the home of Salome, mother of James and John. Together they gathered precious oils and spices. They would observe the Sabbath, but the day after, at dawn, they would proceed to the tomb to render one last service to their Lord.

In the morning, as the sun lighted the east, Mary, Salome, and a few others stole through the quiet streets carrying their small pouch.

"Who will roll away the stone?" one whispered as they rounded the last corner. Mary looked up and gasped. The stone was moved!

Slowly they entered, fearful of what they might see. Before them was a young man in a white robe. The dazzling brightness of his garment filled the dark tomb with a diffused light. Mary could not draw away her eyes from his.

The man told them not to fear. He said that Jesus was alive. With urgency, he ordered them to go and tell the disciples. Then he vanished.

"Come!" Salome urged. They gathered their skirts and fled the tomb, eager to tell the men of their astounding encounter.

But when they reached the room where the disciples were hiding, the men laughed at them. "Women's hysterics," one observed. Peter, however, said nothing. He stood and motioned for John, and together they left the house in silence. Mary followed, remaining in the shadows.

John arrived at the tomb first, but he hesitated at the opening. Then Peter, panting from his run up the hill, rushed into the tomb. Mary waited, quietly watching from behind a gnarled olive tree. In a few moments, Peter and John emerged from the tomb, arguing over the meaning of what they had seen. Had someone stolen the body? Had Jesus risen from the dead?

They never saw Mary as they rushed back to tell the others what they had seen. Feeling abandoned, Mary wept. She stepped over to the tomb for one last look inside. Through her tears she saw two young men. When one asked gently why she cried, she replied, "They have taken my Lord away and I do not know where they have put him." She looked at the men imploringly and saw their focus move from her to something beyond.

Spinning around, fearful that the Roman soldiers had returned, Mary stood face to face with a man dressed in the simple clothes of a laborer. Supposing him to be the gardener, she hastily attempted to dry her eyes.

"Woman," said the stranger, "why are you crying? Who is it that you seek?"

"Oh please, sir, if you have carried away his body, please tell me where you have put him and I will get him."

The gardener's dark eyes softened, and a smile played at his lips. "Mary . . ." was all that he said.

In that instant she knew it was he! Joy pierced her heart. She fell at his feet, crying, "Teacher!"

Gently, he stroked her hair and then helped her to her feet. He explained to her how he must return to the Father, how she could not cling to him any longer. Seeing her despair, he assured her, however, that God would be forever with her as a father is with a beloved child. Then he told her to go and tell the disciples the good news.

Master and servant parted once more, but this time with joy, not sorrow. Mary's feet seemed to have wings as she ran to tell the disciples she had seen and talked to the Lord. Some listened to her tale and believed it; some still doubted. But this mattered little to Mary of Magdala. For she had seen and touched the living God, the resurrected Jesus. That was the reality. There was now hope after despair, laughter after tears, freedom after slavery. There was truly life after death.

Pamela Kennedy is a freelance writer of short stories, articles, essays, and children's books. Married to a naval officer and mother of three children, she has made her home on both U.S. coasts and currently resides in Hawaii. She draws her material from her own experiences and memories, adding bits of imagination to create a story or mood.

Easter Lily Symbol

J. Harold Gwynne

Bright symbol of the Risen One,
    Lift high your chalice fair;
Proclaim again the wondrous news
    Upon the springtime air!

Glad tidings of the risen Lord
    Reveal to all mankind,
That those who put their trust in Him
    New life and hope may find.

Speak through your beauty, chaste and pure,
    Of Christ's own righteousness;
Of peace and joy and holy love,
    He gives our lives to bless.

Lift up our minds to think of Him
    Who died our souls to save;
Who by His rising up again
    Has conquered death and grave.

Inspire our hearts with purest praise
    To our God above
Who binds His people to Himself
    With everlasting love!

50 YEARS AGO

The American Louvre

The United States will arrive at a new period in the world of art when the doors of the National Gallery of Art in Washington swing open on March 17. Americans will then begin to enjoy for the first time a vast collection of the work of the masters, purchased by great private fortunes and passed along to the public in a mammoth marble gallery referred to as the "American Louvre."

Donor of the $15,000,000 gallery and contributor of the costly paintings and sculpture was Andrew W. Mellon, Pittsburgh millionaire, Secretary of the U. S. Treasury under three presidents, and former ambassador to the Court of St. James. It was he who picked the site on Constitution Avenue at the foot of Capitol Hill,

approved John Russel Pope's design, and specified that the "entire public shall forever have access" to the gallery.

As a result, the National Gallery, accepted by Congress and supervised by a board of trustees headed by the chief justicc of thc Unitcd States, will be open to the public without admission charge every day in the year except Christmas and New Year's Day.

As a nucleus for the national art collection, Mr. Mellon donated 126 paintings and 21 sculptures. To these have already been added 375 paintings and 18 sculptures from the Italian collection of Samuel H. Kress, New York chain store merchant. Joseph E. Widener, Philadelphia traction magnate and philanthropist, has

announced that his family's private collection, variously valued at $12,000,000 to $50,000,000 will go to the National Gallery eventually.

The Mellon collection contains paintings dating back to the early Byzantine and up to the American masters—John Singleton Copley, Benjamin West, Gilbert Stuart, and Edward Savage.

Outstanding in the collection are: one of Boticelli's greatest works, "The Adoration of the Magi"; the "Annunciation", by John Van Eyck, one of the founders of the English school and a pioneer in oil painting; nine Rembrandts, including "A Polish Nobleman", once the property of Catherine II of Russia; three of the works of Vermeer, including the remarkable tiny portrait of "The Girl with the Red Hat", and Hans Holbein, the Younger's, portrait of Edward IV as Prince of Wales.

The gallery itself, rivaling the U. S. Capitol in size, will provide five and one half acres and one hundred separate rooms for exhibitions, in addition to lecture rooms, and an art reference library.

The structure is built of 800 tons of rosy Tennessee marble, shading to pure white in the Pantheon-type dome. Inside, plaster, stone, and textiles furnish backdrops for the Italian masters; oak paneling for the Dutch and Flemish. The dark green marble for the 24 rotunda columns was brought over from Italy in the last cargo ship leaving the Mediterranean at the outbreak of war. Daylight will be diffused from the ceiling through sanded, shatterproof glass. An air-conditioning system will aid preservation.

Originally printed in *The Christian Science Monitor Magazine*, March 1941.

Photo Overleaf
TULIP FARM IN HOLLAND
M. Thonig/H. Armstrong Roberts

Andrew W. Mellon and the National Gallery of Art

March 17, 1941, was a blustery, cold day in Washington, D. C. Despite winter's stubborn grip on the weather, however, it was a spring-like mood that seized the large crowd gathered on the Mall at Sixth Street. They had come together that gray March day to celebrate a wonderful new beginning: the opening of the just-completed National Gallery of Art.

Among the nearly 10,000 gathered were some of the most prominent and powerful men and women in the United States. President and Eleanor Roosevelt were there, as were members of the President's cabinet, justices of the Supreme Court, and a majority of both houses of Congress. These leaders of government were joined by leaders of the art world. All had turned out to witness the unveiling of this new American treasure.

Yet despite the number and importance of those gathered, the absence of a single man was felt by all. Andrew W. Mellon—the man whose vision, generosity, and tireless commitment had made the National Gallery a reality—had died in 1937. For Mellon, Secretary of the Treasury under three presidents and former Ambassador to Great Britain, an American art museum to rival France's Louvre and England's own National Gallery had been a consuming goal. He had devoted much of the latter part of his life and an abundance of his huge personal fortune to making the gallery a reality.

Mellon had been the consummate art collector. He had both the educated taste to recognize lasting quality and the financial means to make money no object in pursuit of such quality. Nothing seemed out of his reach. His reputation, his nearly unlimited assets, and a network of agents across the globe guaranteed that if an important painting became available, Andrew Mellon would have the opportunity to buy it.

Such opportunities were not wasted. In 1931, with no more than a few phone calls from his office in Washington, Mellon rescued Goya's *Marquesa de Pontejas y Miraflores* from the threat of revolution in Spain and secured it for his own collection. And when Leningrad's Hermitage Gallery sent out word that it would sell its paintings and sculptures to keep them out of the hands of the Bolsheviks, Mellon again activated his network. The result was a group of twenty-one paintings for the future National Gallery, among them Boticelli's *Adoration of the Magi* and Raphael's *Alba Madonna*.

In this manner, Mellon gathered masterpieces from around the world. And in similar fashion, he created a gallery to house them. He chose the site on Sixth Street and paid for its acquisition. He commissioned architect James Russell Pope and worked alongside him on every detail of the building's design. He chose the perfect pink Tennessee marble for the exterior walls and just the right shade of oak panelling on which to hang the Rembrandts. Leaving no detail to chance, Mellon died with the assurance that his plans for the Gallery would be carried out exactly as he had directed.

Andrew Mellon created the National Gallery from conception to completion with an almost fanatical single-minded devotion. At times he seemed the selfless philanthropist, committed to the ideal of public access to the great masterpieces of art. But just as frequently his actions portrayed a rich and powerful man enthralled by his own financial muscle. His search for paintings and sculptures covered the globe and he spent millions without a second thought. But in the end, he gave it all away, not to a gallery that bore his name, but to a public gallery, open free of charge and administered by a government board.

Like the great artists whose works hang on the Gallery's walls, Mellon was driven by a powerful vision and an unshakable belief that he was the one man to fulfill that vision. If he was motivated by the quest for immortality—as all great artists must be to some extent—he was also blessed with the insight to understand that his great fortune alone was powerless to fulfill that quest. Mellon used his money and power like an artist's paint and brush; the National Gallery was his own creation, his own masterpiece.

And this is what made March 17, 1941, such a special day for all who gathered on the Mall. For on that cold day when the biting wind served as a reminder of the cycles of nature that govern our lives, the National Gallery was dedicated as a monument to man's creativity, one quality that binds generations and cultures and allows mankind to take a stand against the destructive forces of time.

Lord,
Make Me Strong

Jessie Rose Gates

There is a peace that
    cometh after sorrow,
Of hope surrendered,
    not hope fulfilled;
A peace that looketh
    not upon tomorrow,
But calmly on the tempest
    that is stilled.

A peace which lives not now
    in joy's excesses,
Nor in the happy life
    of love secure;
But in the unerring strength
    the heart possesses
Of conflicts won
    while learning to endure.

A peace there is
    in sacrifice secluded;
A life subdued, from will
    and passion free,
'Tis not the peace which over
    Eden brooded,
But that which triumphed
    in Gethsemane.

BITS & PIECES

• • • • • • • • • • • • • • • • • • •

The Lord is my light and my salvation; whom shall I fear? The Lord is the strength of my life; of whom shall I be afraid?

Psalm 27:1

Behold, we know not anything;
I can but trust that good shall fall
At last—far off—at last, to all,
And every winter change to spring.

Alfred, Lord Tennyson

Thou art my way; I wander, if thou fly;
Thou art my light; if hid, how blind am I!
Thou art my life; if thou withdraw, I die.

Francis Quarles

Ring in the valiant man and free,
The longer heart, the kindlier hand;
Ring out the darkness of the land;
Ring in the Christ that is to be.

Alfred, Lord Tennyson

Whither shall I go from thy spirit: or whither shall I go from thy presence? If I climb up into the heaven, thou art there; if I go down to hell, thou art there also. If I take the wings of the morning and remain in the uttermost parts of the sea, even then shall thy hand lead me, and thy right hand shall hold me. If I say peradventure the darkness shall cover me; then shall my night be turned to day. Yea, the darkness is no darkness with thee, but night is as clear as the day: the darkness and light to thee are both alike.

Prayer Book, 1662

Walk in the light and thou shalt see thy path, though thorny, bright; for God, by grace, shall dwell in thee, and God himself is light.

Bruce Barton

Despondency is ingratitude; hope is God's worship.

Henry Ward Beecher

Considering the unforeseen events of this world, we should be taught that no human condition should inspire men with absolute despair.

Henry Fielding

EASTER IN NEW ENGLAND

Rose Koralewsky

There is no death! Life is triumphant ever!
Though wintry gales still sweep across the plain,
Though drifts still lurk unmelted
    on the mountains,
And blue spring skies grow dark
    with sleet and rain,

Forsythia drips with gold despite the snowflakes,
And violets wink bright eyes 'mid
    whitened grass:
The robin's carol yields not to this tempest,
The bluebird murmurs that this too will pass.

Perennial miracle of Life's renewal,
How manifest to us this holy day!
Again we stand in silence and in wonder—
And from our hearts the stone is rolled away.

76

Consolation

Dorothy H. Cross

There is never a day so dreary
But God can make it bright,
And unto the soul that trusts Him,
He giveth songs in the night.

There is never a path so hidden,
But God can lead the way,
If we seek for the Spirit's guidance
And patiently wait and pray.

There is never a cross so heavy
But the nail-scarred hands are there

Outstretched in tender compassion
The burden to help us bear.

There is never a heart so broken,
But the loving Lord can heal
The heart that was pierced on Calvary
Dost still for His loved ones feel.

There is never a life so darkened,
So hopeless and unblessed,
But may be filled with the light of God
And enter His promised rest.

There is never a sin or sorrow,
There is never a care or loss,
But we may bring to Jesus
And leave at the foot of the cross.

Readers' Forum

I have been getting Ideals *for so long I can't remember. But one thing is for sure, I would never be without them. When I am sick they make me feel better, and when I am blue they make me feel happy. If I only had one book to have in my home,* Ideals *would be it.*

Mrs. Patsy Walsfield
Winfield, Illinois

I work in a school and use your magazine for most of my bulletin boards. I don't know what I would do without it. Each month I go through my old Ideals *and settle on a good theme, then continue to find poems or stories to elaborate on my theme. Then I cut flowers, butterflies, borders, etc. to complete my board. Everyone looks forward to my creation each month.*

Letitia Chukas
Port Chester, New York

I have subscribed to Ideals *for many years. To me it is the most beautiful publication in print. I enjoyed seeing the pictures of the cats in the Country issue . . . I am enclosing pictures of my own animal family. Heidi is my two-year-old Shetland Sheepdog. Her cute habit is gathering all her toys and putting them in my lap.*

Gloria Ann Forney
Battle Creek, Michigan